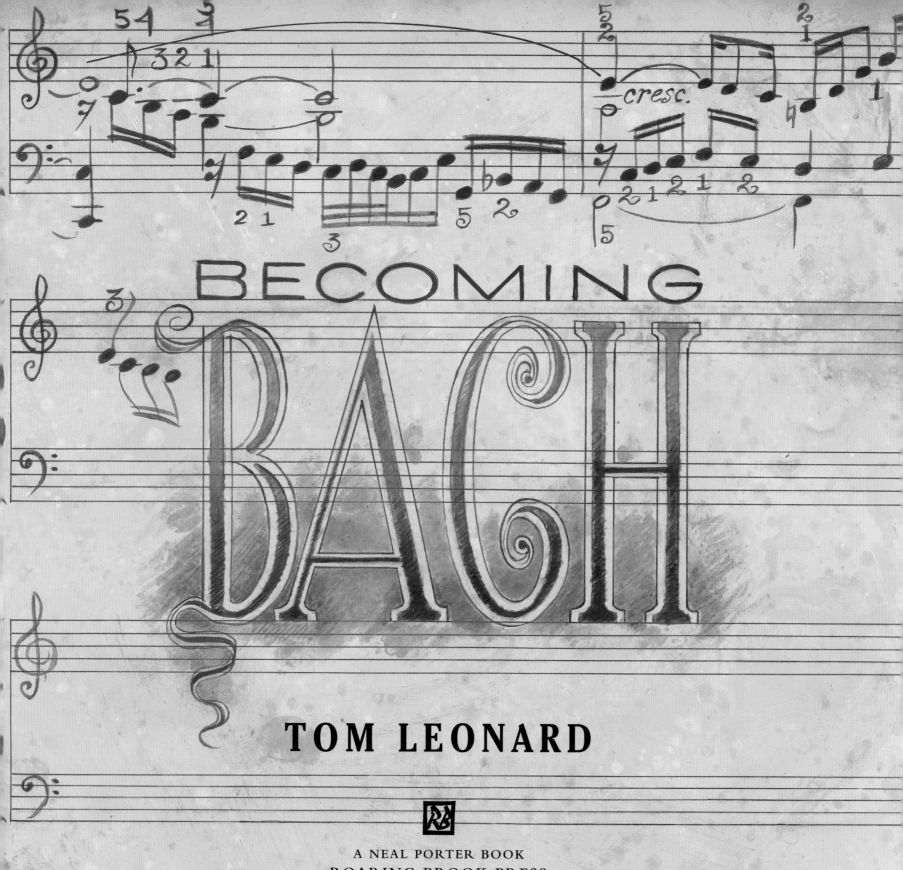

BECOMING BACH

TOM LEONARD

A NEAL PORTER BOOK
ROARING BROOK PRESS
NEW YORK

Thanks to Neal and Jennifer for the opportunity.
Thanks to Carsten Skarke and Karen Ploucqet, and their son Ian (the young Bach),
Christine Koutnik, Anne Lambelet, Alice Krieg, and Kristen Miller for modeling for me.
Thanks to all my family who have always encouraged me. Thanks to all the artists and musicians
that inspired me in this project. Antoine Watteau (for color and musical picnics),
Pieter Bruegel (for snowy landscapes), the history of illustration class
that I teach at UArts in Philadelphia (for unlimited visual options),
Wilson McLean (for being a continual source of inspiration),
and, of course, Johann Sebastian Bach, who brought me here.

Copyright © 2017 by Tom Leonard
A Neal Porter Book
Published by Roaring Brook Press
Roaring Brook Press is a division of Holtzbrinck Publishing
Holdings Limited Partnership
175 Fifth Avenue, New York, New York 10010
The art for this book was created using acrylic paint on illustration board.
mackids.com

Library of Congress Cataloging-in-Publication Data

Names: Leonard, Thomas, 1955–
Title: Becoming Bach / Tom Leonard.
Description: First edition. | New York : Roaring Brook Press, 2017. | "A Neal
    Porter Book."
Identifiers: LCCN 2016025023 | ISBN 9781626722866 (hardcover)
Subjects: LCSH: Bach, Johann Sebastian, 1685–1750—Juvenile literature. |
    Composers—Germany—Biography—Juvenile literature.
Classification: LCC ML3930.B2 L46 2017 | DDC 780.92 [B] —dc23
LC record available at https://lccn.loc.gov/2016025023

Our books may be purchased in bulk for promotional, educational, or business use. Please
contact your local bookseller or the Macmillan Corporate and Premium Sales Department
at (800) 221-7945 ext. 5442 or by e-mail at MacmillanSpecialMarkets@macmillan.com.

First edition 2017
Printed in China by RR Donnelley Asia Printing Solutions Ltd., Dongguan City, Guangdong Province
2   4   6   8   10   9   7   5   3   1

For three strong women without whom this book wouldn't exist:
my mother, Theresa, my agent, Libby, and my wife and muse, Rose.

There was always
music.

Music was always being played.

When it wasn't being played, I heard it in my head.

JOHANN SEBASTIAN BACH
AGE 1

VIET BACH

HEINRICH B

JOHANN JACOB BACH

JOHANN CHRISTOPH BACH

MARIA ELISABETH LÄMMERHIRT

My family had been musicians for over two hundred years.
In our part of Germany, musicians were called bachs.

I always wanted
to be a bach.

We would bring our instruments
and play and sing on a hillside.
Even our picnics had music.

and the organ.

the flute,

And I
sang
in my
strongest
voice.

After mother and
father went to
heaven,

I needed to say things but words weren't enough.

Ohrdruf

~ 1694 ~

I walked over thirty miles with my brother,
Johann Jacob, to live with our oldest
brother, Johann Christoph.
He taught me music.

I loved to copy music, but my brother hid the hard music from me. I found it when he was sleeping at night and copied it.

All of it.

The music made patterns on the page.

The patterns made music when you played them.

Patterns like the designs on my mother's dress.
Patterns like the ripples on the surface of the river.

New sounds, happy sounds, quiet sounds, yellow sounds, red sounds, blue sounds.

All the sounds in my head.

I needed to make patterns, so I wrote music.
Patterns of sound. Patterns of invention.
Just seven notes. Every note made a different sound.

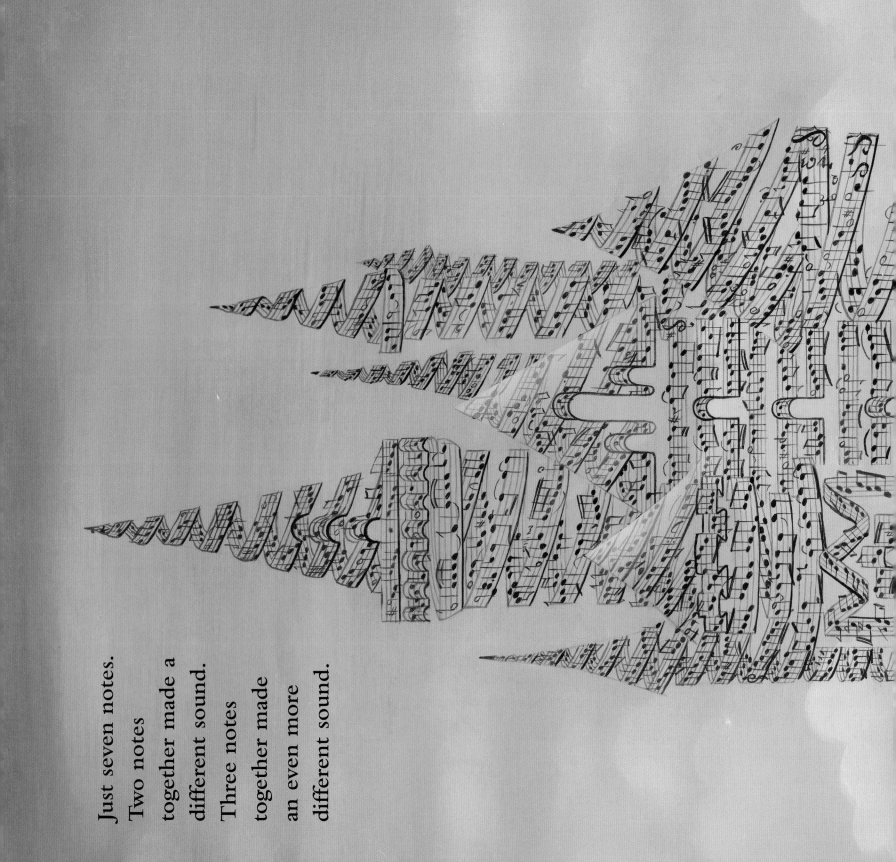

Just seven notes.
Two notes
together made a
different sound.
Three notes
together made
an even more
different sound.

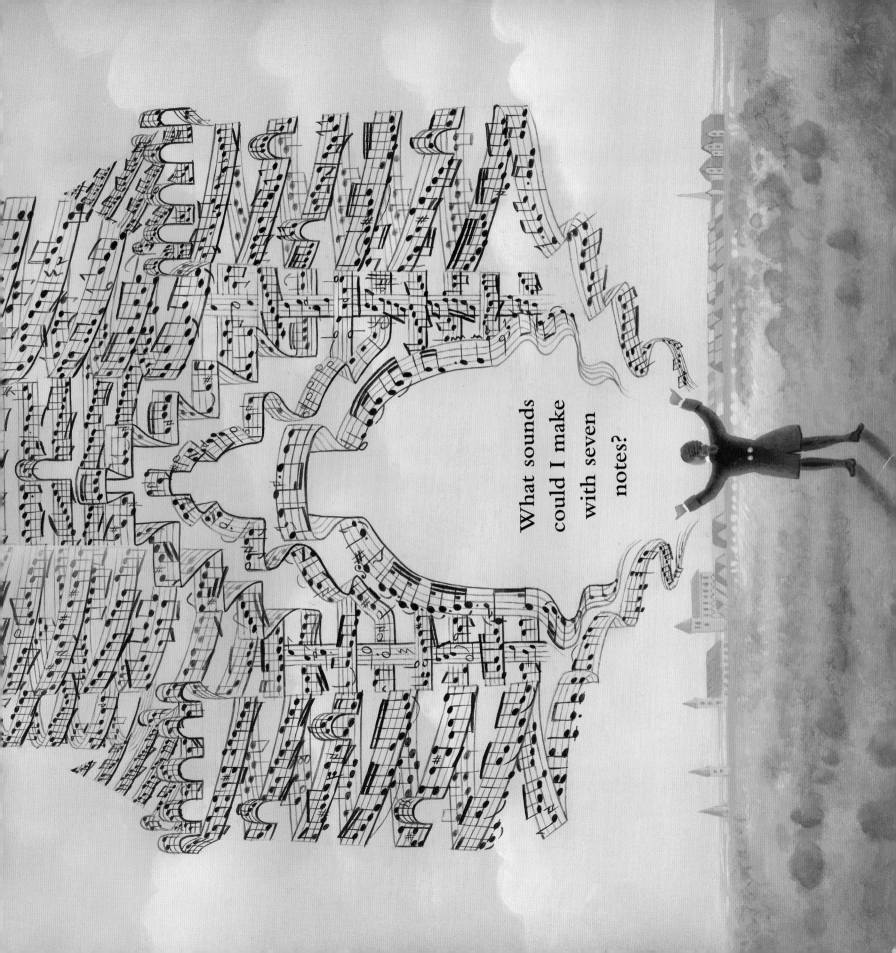

I saw patterns everywhere I looked.

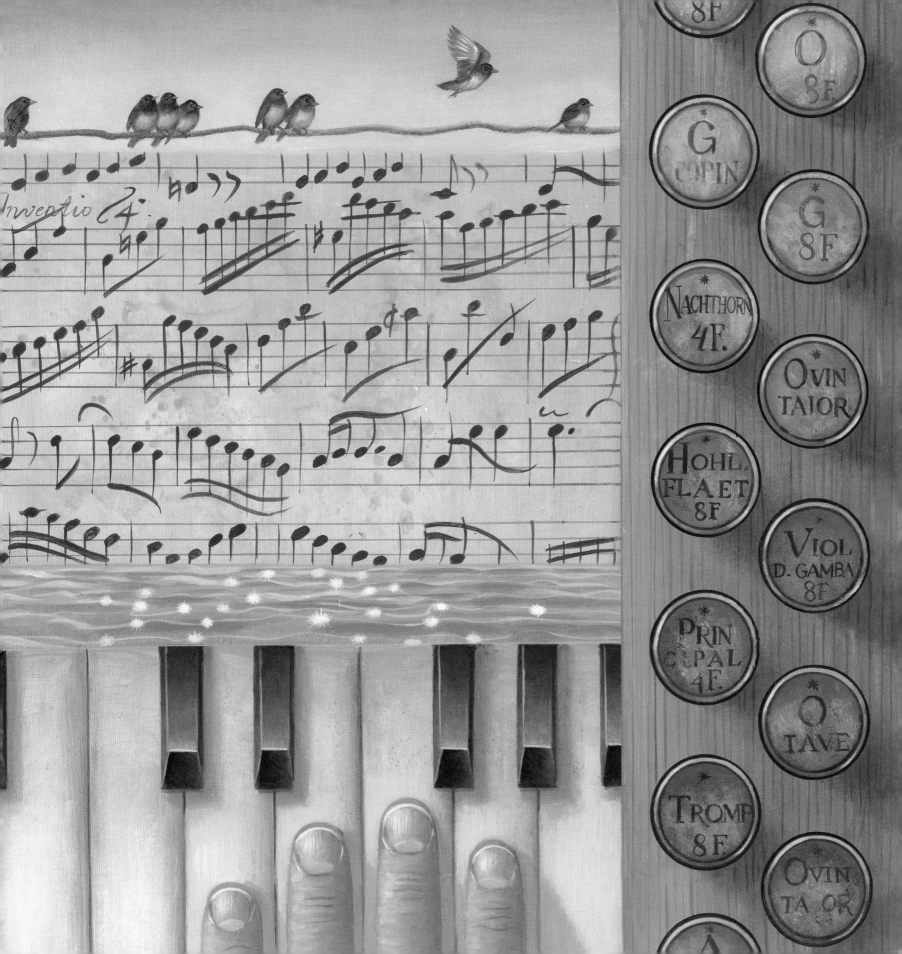

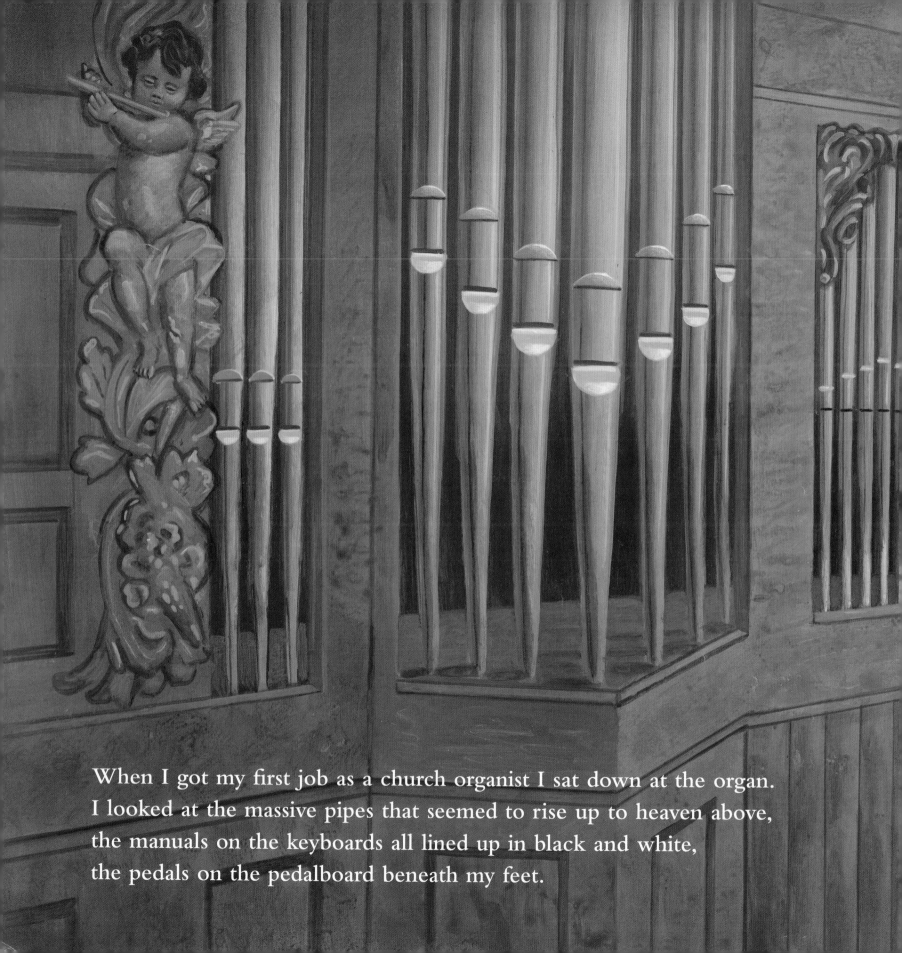

When I got my first job as a church organist I sat down at the organ.
I looked at the massive pipes that seemed to rise up to heaven above,
the manuals on the keyboards all lined up in black and white,
the pedals on the pedalboard beneath my feet.

I looked at the
stops, in rows like
notes on a page.
I pulled out all
the stops.

And I produced the largest sound possible.
A sound that could be heard for miles.
It was a mighty sound. It was a sound that would be heard forever.
It was the sound in my head.

It was then that I knew I had become a bach.
Johann Sebastian Bach.

Johann Sebastian Bach
1685–1750

Born in 1685 in Eisenach, Germany, young Sebastian Bach was a serious boy who loved music. At the age of nine his mother died, followed six months later by his father. Though he was orphaned, he had seven older siblings and was taken under the care of his older brother, Johann Christoph. Christoph gave Sebastian lessons in music.

When he was eighteen he was appointed as violinist in the band of the Duke of Weimar in Mühlhausen, Germany, but Sebastian's true love was the organ. He would watch how organs were built. He would design organs. He would test organs. A year later he became organist and choir director at the town of Arnstadt. His position at Arnstadt didn't last long, however, as the young man was prone to writing music of "strange sounds" and "strange variations," which upset the traditional church authorities. He even allowed a woman, Maria Barbara, to sing in the choir, which was not allowed.

He married Maria and moved from Mühlhausen, where he wrote his first cantatas (longer pieces of music for singers, the organ, and the orchestra), back to Weimar where he continued to write, often pulling from the dramatic flourishes in Italian music. Soon he was experimenting by layering harmonies on top of harmonies, giving his music an emotional resonance that helped establish his name as a master.

Prince Leopold of Köthen persuaded Bach to work privately for him, and there Bach perfected a new technique. Organ players rarely used the thumb and the fourth finger at all. Bach used all five fingers. It was said, "His fingers were all equal strength, all equally able to play with the finest precision. His feet seemed to fly across the pedals as if they were winged, and mighty sounds were heard."

After three years at Köthen, Bach took a trip with Prince Leopold. When he returned home, he found that his beloved wife was dead and buried, leaving behind four children (three had died in infancy). Bach was a man of deep emotions and few words. His suffering would find a voice in music, as it always had.

Within a year, he met Anna Magdalena Wilcke. She loved flowers, music, children, and Bach. They soon married and together had thirteen children.

Over time, Bach tired of Köthen. He left to become cantor to the school of St. Thomas in Leipzig. He would stay there until the end of his life. He now turned his attention to church music and his writing continued to blossom. He wrote songs for religious ceremonies, led the church choir, and played the organ. But Bach wasn't satisfied. He was over-worked and underpaid, but his dedication never faltered.

Bach had never traveled more than two hundred miles from where he was born. During the latter years of his life he withdrew inward, creating some of the most profound music ever written. His energy was used for the highest expressions of musical imagination: the Mass in B Minor; the *Canonic Variations*; the *Goldberg Variations*; *The Musical Offering*; and his last great work that summarized all the methods he had perfected, *The Art of Fugue*.

Bach had a life-long habit of working in poor light and now, as an older man, his eyesight was failing. Then on the morning of July 28, 1750, he woke up to see quite clearly again. He saw Anna and his children around his bed. Later that evening he had a stroke and passed away.

Four of Bach's sons went on to successful musical careers. During his lifetime, Bach's son Carl Philipp Emanuel Bach was considered the superior composer. After his death Johann Sebastian Bach's reputation as a composer, at first, declined. He was remembered more as a player and a teacher. His sons and his students kept his memory partially alive.

But one hundred years after his death, his reputation began reemerging slowly, until now, when many regard him as the greatest composer of all time.

A NOTE FROM THE AUTHOR

As a child I heard my mother play Bach's music on the piano. I immediately felt that Bach was talking to me. That's me as a child wearing the Bach shirt at the end of this book.

Bach's music always seemed to be played at occasions of deep emotion: holidays, weddings, and funerals. It played at my own wedding.

How did simple black dots on a page result in music of such passion and emotion? Mathematical patterns in search of a soul. Bach understood things that I never could.

He lived a humble life in a small German town, far from the limelight. And yet, he evoked the depths and passions of human existence like no other person. Bach's music is the sound of our souls.

I chose to write *Becoming Bach* in the first person to give the story a sense of immediacy; though the story is his, the words are mine.

SUGGESTED LISTENING

Prelude No. 1 in C Major from *The Well-Tempered Clavier*, Book 1, BWV 846

Aria from the *Goldberg Variations*, BWV 988

Cantata, BWV 147, *Jesu, Joy of Man's Desiring*

Arioso from Cantata, BWV 156, Adagio

Cantata, BWV 140, Sleepers Awake

Contrapunctus 9 from *The Art of Fugue*, BWV 1080

Toccata and Fugue in D Minor, BWV 565

Brandenburg Concerto No. 2 in F Major, first movement, BWV 1047

Concerto for Two Violins in D Minor, BWV 1043

Mass in B Minor, BWV 232

St. Matthew Passion, Part 1, Chor mit choral, BWV 244

Magnificat in D Major, BWV 243

SOURCES

Borsch-Supan, Helmut. *Antoine Watteau: Masters of French Art*. Kohn, Germany: Konemann, 2001.

Cencetti, Greta. *Bach. The World of Composers*. Columbus, Ohio: Peter Bedrick Books, 2002.

Dreyfus, Laurence. *Bach and the Patterns of Invention*. Boston: Harvard University Press, 2004.

Elie, Paul. *Reinventing Bach*. New York: Farrar, Straus and Giroux, 2012.

Erikson, Raymond, ed. *The Worlds of Johann Sebastian Bach*. New York: Amadeus Press, 2009.

Gardiner, John Eliot. *Bach: Music in the Castle of Heaven*. New York: Alfred A. Knopf, 2013.

Getzinger, Donna, & Daniel Felsenfeld. *Johann Sebastian Bach and the Art of Baroque Music*. Greensboro, North Carolina: Morgan Reynolds, 2004.

Greene, Carol. *Johann Sebastian Bach: Great Man of Music*. Rookie Biographies. Chicago: Children's Press, 1992.

WEBSITES

Great Composers: Bach, BBC, 1997
youtube.com/watch?v=MkKd1fjgqKI

The Face of Bach
bach-cantatas.com

notablebiographies.com/Ba-Be/Bach-Johann-Sebastian.html

jsbach.org/timeline.html

baroquemusic.org/bqxjsbach.html